THIS LAND CALLED AMERICA: **ARKANSAS**

CREATIVE EDUCATION

Published by Creative Education
P.O. Box 227, Mankato, Minnesota 56002
Creative Education is an imprint of The Creative Company
www.thecreativecompany.us

Book and cover design by Blue Design (www.bluedes.com)
Art direction by Rita Marshall
Printed in the United States of America

Photographs by Corbis (Buddy Mays, John Wigmore), Getty Images
(Altrendo Nature, American School, Thomas S. England//Time Life
Pictures, Focus on Sport, Imagno, David McNew, Michael Ochs Ar-
chives, Brian Miller/Ovoworks/Ovoworks/Time Life Pictures, Francis
Miller//Time Life Pictures, MPI, Panoramic Images, Ken Ross, Ryan/
Beyer, Joel Sartore, Harrison Shull, Stephen B. Thornton, Mark Wilson)

Library of Congress Cataloging-in-Publication Data
Shofner, Shawndra.
Arkansas / by Shawndra Shofner.
p. cm. — (This land called America)
Includes bibliographical references and index.
ISBN 978-1-58341-629-7
1. Arkansas—Juvenile literature. I. Title. II. Series.
F411.3.S55 2007
976.7—dc22   2007008491

First Edition
9 8 7 6 5 4 3 2 1

This Land Called America

ARKANSAS

Shawndra Shofner

Arkansas

SHAWNDRA SHOFNER

TALL PINE TREES SWAY IN THE BREEZE AROUND
WHAT LOOKS LIKE A PLOWED FARMER'S FIELD.
ALL DAY LONG, PEOPLE PICK THROUGH THE
CLUMPY DIRT. ONE FAMILY WORKS TOGETHER,
DIGGING AND SIFTING. A GROUP OF TEENS
CARRYING SHOVELS DASH TO A HOLE THEY
STARTED THE DAY BEFORE. AN OLDER MAN WALKS
SLOWLY, POKING THE DIRT WITH HIS CANE. THIS
IS CRATER OF DIAMONDS STATE PARK NEAR
MURFREESBORO, ARKANSAS. IT IS THE ONLY
PLACE IN THE WORLD WHERE PEOPLE ARE INVITED
TO SEARCH FOR DIAMONDS AND TO KEEP ANY
THEY FIND. AND CHANCES ARE GOOD THAT AT
LEAST ONE DIAMOND WILL BE FOUND BY A LUCKY
ROCKHOUND IN ARKANSAS EVERY DAY.

YEAR
1541   Spanish explorer Hernando de Soto crosses the Mississippi River into what is now Arkansas.
EVENT

- 5 -

Territory Travelers

In 1541, Spanish explorer Hernando de Soto crossed the Mississippi River into what is now Arkansas. He and his soldiers were looking for gold, but they would not find any. They likely came upon American Indian villages of the Parkin and Tula people. In May of the next year, de Soto reportedly died on the river's bank near present-day Lake Village, Arkansas.

Hernando de Soto

Early explorers such as Hernando de Soto (left) saw the rocky bluff country (opposite) near the Mississippi River that would become Arkansas.

French explorers Jacques Marquette and Louis Jolliet canoed down the Mississippi River in 1673. They were looking for the Pacific Ocean. They met the Quapaw Indians near the Arkansas River. The Indians told the explorers that the Mississippi flowed to the Gulf of Mexico, not the Pacific Ocean. The Indians also warned them of unfriendly tribes to the south, so Marquette and Jolliet returned north.

In 1682, another French explorer, René-Robert de La Salle, brought explorers and soldiers from Canada to the Gulf of Mexico. He claimed all of the land west of the Mississippi River

YEAR
1673 Jacques Marquette and Louis Jolliet are the first French explorers in Arkansas Territory.
EVENT

Arkansas forests provided early military posts and settlements with food and building materials.

to the Rocky Mountains and north from the Gulf of Mexico to Canada for France. He named the territory Louisiana after France's King Louis XIV. Henri de Tonti, a French adventurer, traveled with La Salle. He set up Arkansas Post at the mouth of the Arkansas River. The post was the first European settlement in what is now Arkansas.

France gave the Louisiana Territory to Spain in 1763. But in 1800, France's emperor, Napoleon Bonaparte, took it back by force. Three years later, Bonaparte sold the 828,000 square miles (2,144,520 sq km) of land to the United States. The Louisiana Purchase doubled the size of the U.S.

Arkansas Post became the capital of the Arkansas Territory in 1819. Settlers moved to the new territory and lived in log houses with dirt or wood floors. They hunted bear, deer, rabbits, and waterfowl. The people also grew corn and cotton in the rich soil in the east. African American slaves worked on many large farms called plantations.

An Arkansas lawyer named Ambrose H. Sevier is known as the "Father of Arkansas Statehood." He was elected as the territory's delegate, or spokesperson, to the U.S. Congress in 1828. Sevier convinced Congress to admit Arkansas as the 25th state on June 15, 1836. The next year, Sevier became the state's first senator.

YEAR

1740   Pierre de Bienville, the governor of the Louisiana Territory, introduces cotton to the Mississippi River Valley.

EVENT

At the Battle of Pea Ridge, Union troops were outnumbered by about 5,000 men but still emerged victorious.

YEAR
1803 The U.S. negotiates with France for the Louisiana Purchase. The land includes Arkansas.
EVENT

- 10 -

Cotton farmers in Arkansas and other parts of the South relied on slave labor to supply their goods to other states and countries. Many people in northern states disagreed with the practice of slavery, though. They wanted all slaves to be set free. In an effort to hold on to their rights to own slaves, 11 southern states, including Arkansas, withdrew from the Union, or northern states. They formed the Confederate States of America. The American Civil War between the North and South began in April 1861.

Several decisive battles, such as the Battle of Pea Ridge, were fought in Arkansas during the Civil War. However, the South lost most of them, including Pea Ridge, which was fought in northwestern Arkansas on March 7 and 8, 1862. Less than a year later, Union troops took over Arkansas Post. In 1865, the Union claimed final victory, and slaves were given their freedom. Congress readmitted Arkansas to the Union in 1868, and the South began to rebuild itself.

Sometimes protected by Union soldiers, large groups of freed slaves made their way north starting in 1863.

In a Natural State

Six states surround Arkansas. Missouri forms the northern border. Louisiana is to the south. The Mississippi River forms most of the eastern border, along with Missouri, Tennessee, and Mississippi. Texas and Oklahoma lie to the west.

The five land areas of Arkansas reveal why it is nicknamed the "Natural State." The Mississippi Alluvial Plain is found in the eastern third of the state. (Alluvial plains are low-lying areas in which rich soil deposits were laid by a river, such as the Mississippi.) From north to south in the western part of the state lie the Ozark Plateau, Arkansas Valley, Ouachita Mountains, and the West Gulf Coastal Plain.

The Mississippi Alluvial Plain is also known as the Delta or Grand Prairie. It stretches from Missouri south to Louisiana. From the Mississippi River, it reaches west as far as Little Rock, Arkansas. This land is mostly flat and swampy. Some farmers grow rice in the wet, fertile soil. Other farmers operate catfish farms. Deer, rabbits, foxes, and bobcats are native to the Plain.

Arkansas' Big Woods covers 550,000 acres (222,577 ha) in the Mississippi Alluvial Plain.

The Arkansas Valley region includes the highest point in the state, Mount Magazine.

YEAR

1810

EVENT

A census finds that more than 1,000 people live in Arkansas, not including American Indians.

M

any birds follow the Mississippi River south when they migrate for the winter. The path they take is called the Mississippi Flyway. The eastern border of Arkansas is in the Mississippi Flyway. Because of its abundance of birds, Arkansas is called the duck-hunting capital of the world. Hunters can also take aim at pheasants and geese.

The Ozark Plateau covers the north-central and northwestern parts of Arkansas. Rocky hills, bluffs, gorges, and ridges make up this scenic area. Waterfalls spill from sandstone and limestone crests. Under the ground are caves, caverns, and even streams. The town of Eureka Springs is known for its 63 cold springs. The Boston Mountains rise in the southern part

Thought to have been extinct, the ivory-billed woodpecker, relative of the pileated woodpecker (above), was found in 2005 near Bayou Bartholomew (opposite) in eastern Arkansas.

Territorial leader Ambrose H. Sevier helps Arkansas become the 25th state on June 15.

Bird watchers and scientists like to search for rare birds in the wooded areas of Arkansas.

of the Plateau. The mountains' hickory forests are home to mink, raccoons, skunks, weasels, and woodchucks.

Coal mines and natural gas wells can be found in the Arkansas Valley south of the Ozark Plateau. The Arkansas River winds through most of the Valley. Mountains called Nebo, Petit Jean, and Magazine form what is known as the scenic tri-peaks region. The Cedar Falls waterfall on Petit Jean splashes 95 feet (29 m) down to Cedar Creek. The highest point in the state is Magazine Mountain, which towers 2,753 feet (839 m) above sea level.

The ridges and valleys of the Ouachita Mountains are in west-central Arkansas. This region is rich in quartz crystal and timber. There are 47 springs at Hot Springs Mountain with temperatures that average 143 °F (62 °C). When the Blakely Mountain Dam on the Ouachita River was built in 1953, it created Ouachita Lake. Ouachita is the largest lake in Arkansas.

The West Gulf Coastal Plain covers the southwestern and south-central parts of Arkansas. The low, flat land is covered in pine forests. Harvesting trees for wood products is a major

YEAR

1861   Arkansas joins the Confederate States of America and sends 50,000 troops to the Confederate army.

EVENT

- *16* -

State bird: mockingbird

industry on the Plain. Natural gas, petroleum, and diamonds are found beneath the surface of the Plain.

Temperatures in Arkansas average a humid 81 °F (27 °C) in the summer. Heat streaks in August are common, with temperatures rising above 100 °F (38 °C). Winter temperatures can dip to 0 °F (-18 °C) but average 40 °F (4 °C). About 49 inches (124 cm) of rain falls in the state every year.

In mountainous northern and western Arkansas, rock climbers can find challenging terrain.

Gloria Ray | Terrance Roberts | Melba Patillo

Elizabeth Eckford | Ernest Green | MinniJean Brown

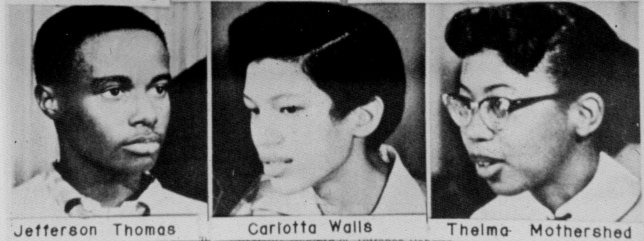

Jefferson Thomas | Carlotta Walls | Thelma Mothershed

THE LITTLE ROCK NINE

The city of Little Rock (opposite) was the scene of a conflict in 1957 that involved nine black students known as "The Little Rock Nine."

Tears and Triumph

People from France came to Arkansas in the 1700s. They brought African American slaves to work on their farms. In the 1800s, settlers from nearby states moved to Arkansas. Many of them were Scottish, Irish, and German. They came to the low and swampy land of the Mississippi Delta because they could buy land cheaply and grow cotton on it. They also brought slaves to work on the big plantations.

Governor Orval Faubus (above, far right) did not want people of different races to mix together.

After the Civil War ended in 1865, African Americans received their freedom. But they were still often treated unfairly. African Americans were forced to use separate rest rooms and drinking fountains. They also had to sit in the backs of buses and give up their seats to white travelers. African American children had to attend separate schools. But in 1954, the U.S. Supreme Court ruled that such separation was against the law, and public schools were ordered to admit all children.

Some Arkansans still wanted to keep white and black students in separate schools. On September 4, 1957, Governor Orval Faubus used the National Guard to stop nine African American students from attending Little Rock's Central High School. Since this went against the Supreme Court's ruling, President Dwight D. Eisenhower stepped in. He gave the students armed bodyguards. The nine students started attending Central High three weeks later.

YEAR

1906 Farmer John Huddleston discovers diamonds on his farm south of Murfreesboro.

EVENT

Many entertainers and artists have come from Arkansas. The famous African American poet, actress, and author Maya Angelou grew up in Stamps. Country singer Johnny Cash was born in Kingsland in 1932. He won 11 Grammy awards in his lifetime. Edward Durell Stone from Fayetteville was a gifted architect. One of his many designs was the John F. Kennedy Center for the Performing Arts in Washington, D.C.

Johnny Cash

Johnny Cash, pictured here around 1960, recorded more than 1,500 songs during his almost 50-year career.

YEAR

1920   In April, oil is discovered near Stephens, marking the start of the Arkansas oil boom.

EVENT

In 1946, Bill Clinton was born in Hope. Raised in Hot Springs, Clinton went on to serve two terms as governor of Arkansas and to become the 42nd president of the U.S. When he was elected president in 1992, Clinton gave his acceptance speech on the steps of Little Rock's Old State House. The Old State House, now a museum, was completed in 1842 and is the oldest surviving state capitol west of the Mississippi.

Professional baseball player Brooks Robinson, who spent his 23-year career with the Baltimore Orioles, was from Little Rock. Named the American League's Most Valuable Player in 1964, he was one of the best third basemen in history.

The year 1978 marked Brooks Robinson's (above) first year of retirement from baseball and Bill Clinton's (opposite) first year as Arkansas' governor.

The U.S.'s first woman senator, Hattie Caraway, is elected to office by Arkansas voters.

Statewide, Arkansas farmers plant and harvest about one million acres (404,686 ha) of cotton each year.

The communities of Little Rock and North Little Rock (above) are thriving on new businesses.

Arkansas farm

Today, some Arkansans mine for bauxite, which is used in making aluminum, near Little Rock. Others work at natural gas and petroleum wells in the southern and western parts of the state. Paper industries, lumber mills, and food processors also employ people. Still, agriculture is the primary industry in Arkansas. Farmers grow rice, soybeans, and cotton. Ranchers raise chickens, turkeys, cattle, and hogs. In recent years, many Hispanic people have moved to Arkansas to work in the poultry industry.

People live in Arkansas because of the low cost of living, opportunities for work, and beautiful natural spaces. Most live in or near 10 of the state's largest cities. Almost 200,000 people live in Little Rock, including many retired people who make the peaceful northwestern part of the state a relaxing place to call home.

YEAR
1957
EVENT

Little Rock high schools temporarily close after nine African American students attempt to attend Central High.

- 25 -

Arkansas Treasures

AMERICAN INDIANS LIVED IN WHAT IS NOW ARKANSAS FOR MORE THAN 10,000 YEARS. THE PLUM BAYOU PEOPLE HAD VILLAGES IN EAST-CENTRAL ARKANSAS. THEY GREW BARLEY, HUNTED, AND GATHERED WILD BERRIES AND NUTS. FIVE OF THE 18 MOUNDS THEY BUILT FOR RELIGIOUS AND SOCIAL PURPOSES CAN STILL BE SEEN AT THE TOLTEC MOUNDS SITE SOUTHEAST OF LITTLE ROCK. ONE MOUND IS 49 FEET (15 M) TALL.

The U.S. Army forced American Indian tribes out of the southeastern states of Georgia, Tennessee, North Carolina, and Alabama in 1838. Thousands died on the 2,200-mile (3,540 km) journey to Oklahoma, traveling through Arkansas on the way. The route is mapped out today as the Trail of Tears National Historic Trail.

American Indians called a place in the Ouachita Mountains the "Valley of the Vapors" because steam rose from 47 boiling springs there. Indians and the first white settlers believed that the springs held mysterious healing powers, which eventually attracted interest from around the world. Soon, the area became known as Hot Springs, the first resort town in the U.S. Hot Springs was also the boyhood home of Bill Clinton, who was U.S. president from 1993 to 2001.

Every June, Arkansans gather for the two-day Pink Tomato Festival in the small southern town of Warren. Tomato lovers can compete in tomato-packing contests or enter the Miss Pink Tomato pageant. They can also eat their fill at the tomato-eating contest, homemade salsa contest, and the all-tomato luncheon. The Pink Tomato Festival celebrated 51 years in 2007. It is the longest-running festival in Arkansas.

The only building in the world built entirely from blocks of pink bauxite is located in Benton, Arkansas. Patients of Dr.

In the caves of Arkansas' Ozarks, people can get close enough to touch the unique rock formations.

Near the northwestern town of Eureka Springs is a glass-filled sanctuary named Thorncrown Chapel.

Dewell Gann Sr. built the building in 1893 to repay him for his services. An imprint of Dr. Gann's foot can be seen on an inside wall, left by the doctor as he rested his foot on it while waiting for patients. In 1946, Dr. Dewell Gann Jr. donated the building to the city of Benton. It became the Gann Museum of Saline County in 1980.

There are numerous state parks scattered around Arkansas, but Crater of Diamonds is perhaps the most unique. Located in the southwestern part of the state, Crater of Diamonds State Park is the only place in the world where the public is invited to mine for diamonds—along with the 40 other types of rocks and minerals that can be found there.

North of Crater of Diamonds is Ouachita National Forest and the Little Missouri River.

Although Arkansas does not have professional sports teams of its own, many successful athletes have come from the state. Hazel Walker was one of the best female basketball players of all time. Born in Oak Hill in 1914, she and her team,

YEAR

1980   A record heat wave produces 20 straight days of temperatures topping 100 °F (38 °C).

EVENT

YEAR

1992   Arkansan William Jefferson "Bill" Clinton is elected as the 42nd president of the U.S.

EVENT

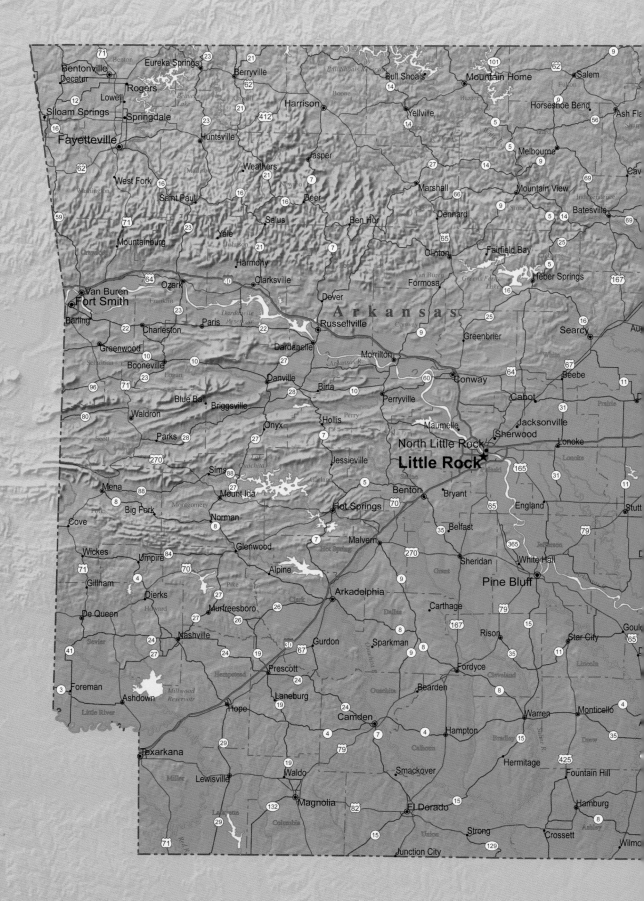

QUICK FACTS

Population: 2,810,872

Largest city: Little Rock (pop. 184,053)

Capital: Little Rock

Entered the union: June 15, 1836

Nickname: Natural State

State flower: apple blossom

State bird: mockingbird

Size: 53,179 sq mi (137,733 sq km)—29th-biggest in U.S.

Major industries: agriculture, manufacturing, mining

the Arkansas Travelers, played against men and won more than 85 percent of their games. Golfer John Daly began his career at Dardanelle High School and the University of Arkansas in Fayetteville. He won the Professional Golfers' Association of America (PGA) championship in 1991.

It is easy to find talented people and beautiful places anywhere in the Natural State. Add in strong industries and profitable farming, and Arkansans have a sure recipe for success. Whether or not they find any diamonds in Crater of Diamonds State Park, those who live in Arkansas count themselves lucky.

YEAR

2002   Wal-Mart, headquartered in Bentonville, becomes the world's largest corporation.

EVENT

- 31 -

BIBLIOGRAPHY

Anything Arkansas. "Encyclopedia of Arkansas." Anything Arkansas Directory. http://www.anythingarkansas.com/arkapedia/pedia/.

Di Piazza, Domenica. *Arkansas*. Minneapolis: Lerner Publications, 2001.

Dregni, Eric. *Midwest Marvels*. Minneapolis: University of Minnesota Press, 2006.

Marshall, Richard, et al. *Explore America*. Washington, D.C.: AAA Publishing, 1996.

National Park Service. "The Battle of Pea Ridge, March 7 & 8, 1862." National Park Service. http://www.nps.gov/archive/peri/battle_intro.htm.

Zenfell, Martha. *Insight Guide United States: On the Road*. Long Island City, NY: Langenscheidt Publishing Group, 2001.

INDEX